# RAINY DAYS

# SHADOW THEATER

## DENNY ROBSON
## AND
## VANESSA BAILEY

## GLOUCESTER PRESS
New York · London · Toronto · Sydney

# CONTENTS

*Design:* David West
Children's Book Design
*Photography:* Roger Vlitos

© Aladdin Books Ltd 1990

*First published in
the United States in 1991 by*
Gloucester Press
387 Park Avenue South
New York, NY 10016

Printed in Belgium

Library of Congress
Cataloging-in-Publication Data

Bailey, Vanessa.
    Shadow theater : games and projects /
    Vanessa Bailey
        p.    cm. -- (Rainy days)
    Includes index.
    Summary: A step-by-step approach to
shadow theater, from hand shadows to
shadows with accessories made from
simple materials.
    ISBN 0-531-17270-8
    1. Shadow shows--Juvenile literature.
2. Shadow puppets--Juvenile literature.
3. Puppet making--Juvenile literature. [ 1.
Shadow shows. 2. Shadow puppets.
3. Puppets. 4. Puppet making.] I. Title.
II. Series: Bailey, Vanessa. Rainy days.
PN1979.S5B24     1991
791.5'3--dc20      90-44630     CIP   AC

# Introduction

Shadow theater is one of the oldest forms of
theater in the world. India and China both have
long traditions of shadow theater. In Indonesia,
the art of Wayang Purwa (*wayang* means
shadow, *purwa* means ancient) grew out of
primitive ancestor worship and is still
performed today. Beautifully painted and gilded
puppets of gods, demons and heroes cast
shadows on a screen telling stories which teach
people how to live wisely.

    This book shows you how to become part of
the world of shadow theater. You can find out
how to have fun creating hand shadows and
how to put on a shadow play using jointed
puppets. With a little imagination, some simple
materials and a bit of practice, you can make
shadows come alive!

These are some of the
materials we used to
make the shadow
puppets in this book.
Once you have made the
puppets, you may find
you have lots of ideas for
creating your own
shadow characters.

# Hand shadows

Hand shadows can be as simple or as complicated as you want to make them. The shadow creatures on the next few pages are quite easy to create, but with a little practice they can be made to act out dramas. Change the position of your fingers and they open and close their eyes. Experiment with different sound effects and move their mouths so that they appear to bark, neigh or screech. They can grow larger and smaller, chase each other or even fight to the death!

To create hand shadows you need a light source behind you and a plain wall in front. You could use a reading lamp, a flashlight or even sunlight. If you don't have a plain white wall, perhaps you could ask a grown-up to pin up a white sheet instead.

RABBIT

DOG

OSTRICH

5

# Hand shadows

ELEPHANT

BIRD

PUNK ROCKER

BABY RABBIT

VULTURE

WOLF

# Hand shadows with props

You can create a whole host of exciting hand shadows by using cut-out cardboard props. Quite simple shapes can prove very effective, like the rooster's comb below, or you can make more intricate cut-outs, like the group of knights doing battle on page 11. For these more complicated shadows, make sure you use a strong light source and have your hands quite close to the wall. That way the shadow will be as clear as possible and you will be able to see all the detail.

**ROOSTER**
This simple cardboard cut-out is the rooster's comb. Glue or tape a loop of cardboard to its base for your finger. You can use your other hand to create the rooster's feathers.

## CROCODILE

Make the crocodile's head in two separate pieces. Cut out an eye and nostril. Glue loops to each piece for your fingers. Your arm provides the crocodile's long body.

## FISHERMAN

The fisherman's head and hat are cut from one piece of cardboard, with a loop for your finger. The rod is a rolled up strip of cardboard, with string for the line to catch the fish.

# Hand shadows with props

## THE BOXERS
These mean-looking boxers are all ready to fight it out. Cut out their heads and boxing gloves and attach loops. Put them on your fingers as shown and let the match begin!

## POP GROUP

The guitarist has long wool hair tied in a pony tail, while the singer's spiky hair is made from string. You could make other members of the band and get a friend to help with the performance.

## KNIGHTS IN ARMOR

With their plumed helmets, shields and swords, these knights are all ready to fight to the death.

# Making a theater

A shadow theater has a translucent screen, which means it lets light shine through. Puppets perform behind the screen so that only the shadow of the figure is seen by the audience. You can make a shadow theater in many different ways. It could be a picture frame with a piece of old sheet stretched across it, or you could cut up a cardboard box, decorate it and tape tracing or wax paper to it.

Our shadow theater below is very simple to make. Cut a circle out of black cardboard, color some appropriate scenery onto tracing paper and glue this to the cardboard. Tie or tape it to a chair and set up the light source.

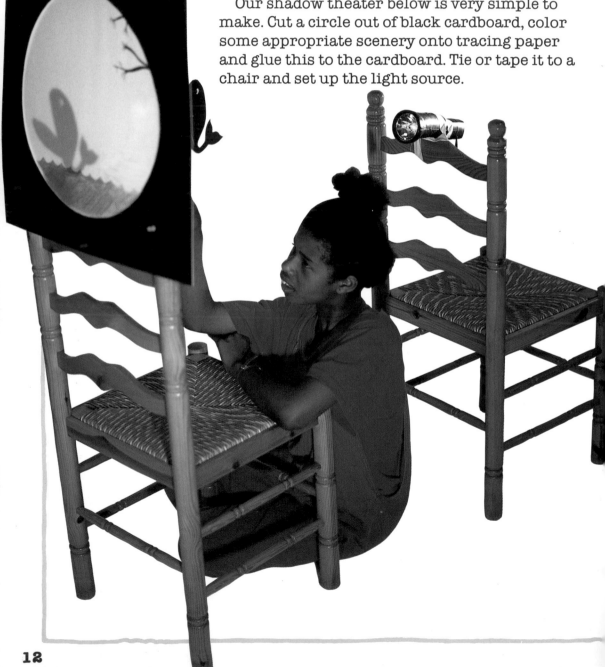

The crocodile looks sinister against a murky swamp screen.

Your hand shadows with their props can also act in the theater if you hold them close to the screen. You could draw a boxing ring on the screen for the fighters to perform in and use a bicycle bell to mark the beginning and end of each round!

The rooster crows against a pink dawn sky.

# Simple puppets

Shadow puppets are flat figures, worked by sticks or strings, that you hold against the screen. Traditional shadow puppets were made out of painted and oiled leather or parchment, but you can make excellent shadow puppets out of thin, stiff cardboard.

It's a good idea to make lots of different puppets for your plays. The figures don't all have to look realistic — you can create scary monsters or creatures with one animal's head and another's body. Use your imagination to make them as funny, fierce, ridiculous or as beautiful as you like.

**DINOSAUR**
This rather fierce-looking stegosaurus is controlled by a stick glued to its back.

**SPIDER**
This big spooky spider with its sharp fangs showing is hanging by a thread behind the screen.

**MONKEY**
Paint your screen to look like a jungle and let the monkey swing through the trees by the thread tied to his tail.

# Jointed puppets

Shadow puppets that appear to move parts of themselves can look very exciting. They can be simple, like the whale whose mouth opens and closes, or clever and complex, like our dancing clown on page 23. There are patterns at the back of the book to help you make the more complicated puppets.

**ORCHESTRA**
You need two people to work this witty puppet, one to operate the conductor, and one the violinists. Join the conductor's arms to his body with a paper fastener. Make loops at either end of the row of violinists, slot in their bows and slide back and forth to make them play!

## SONGBIRD

The bird is made in two parts and is jointed in such a way that its mouth opens and closes as it sings. Use the pattern if you need help.

## WHALE

The whale's jaws are jointed and a thread is attached to the lower jaw. Pull on the thread and the whale opens and closes its mouth.

## SKULL

The skull is made in two pieces, with a stick attached to the lower jaw and another to a framework on the upper jaw. Loosely tie the sticks together and move them up and down to make the skull speak!

# Jointed puppets

**SWINGING MONKEY**
Cut out and assemble the monkey so that the limbs move freely. Thread string through the hands, hold each end and the monkey will swing.

**MISS MUFFET**
Shake the stick supporting Miss Muffet to make her legs and skirt move. Pull on the strings attached to the tops of her arms and her hands go up and down.

## LION AND LION TAMER

Use the patterns to draw the shapes, cut them out and assemble using paper fasteners. Pass a piece of thread through the lion's jaw as shown. Pull and release to make the lion close and open his mouth.

The lion tamer's whip is a piece of string. Tie thread to the tops of his arms and jerk the thread to make him lash out with his whip.

# Colored puppets

Not all shadow puppets cast black shadows. They can also be brightly and beautifully colored. You have already seen that you can create faces on black cardboard puppets by cutting out shapes so that the light shines through. By gluing colored cellophane (candy wrappers are a good source), colored film or tissue across these cut-outs, your puppet can seem more alive. Monsters can have red glinting eyes, kings wear jeweled crowns and dragons become more fantastic.

### GARDEN SCENE
The bright colors of the flower are pieces of cellophane that have been glued to the black cardboard cut-out. The butterfly has been made with cardboard and clear acetate film colored with felt-tip pens.

## DRAGON
This fabulous creature
has been created by
gluing clear acetate film
to the black cardboard
cut-out and then colored
with felt-tip pens.

## BUMBLEBEE
The bee's stripes are
yellow tissue paper. Blue
tissue has been used for
its eyes and a tiny piece
of red makes its nose.

# Jointed colored puppets

Once you have made some shadow puppets, starting with the simple one-piece shapes and experimenting with puppets with moving parts, you are ready to try the more complex colored puppets. Then perhaps you can use these basic techniques to create a whole range of characters of your own.

**JEWELED FISH**
This beautiful creature is made in the same way as the whale (page 17), except that sections have been cut out, and colored film inserted to make it look more exotic.

## DANCING CLOWN

Tie the legs together and the arms together. Then link them with another piece of string. When you pull on the string, the clown will dance!

## SNAKE

The snake is made in separate sections, with each piece tied to the next. You can make it as long as you want, although you may need more sticks to support it.

# The play

You have made your theater, the puppets are ready and now it's time to make the shadows come alive. First you have to decide on your story. Simple stories are easiest for your audience to follow. Decide which puppets will be used and how many helpers you will need. It might even be a good idea to write out a script. Color the scenery and don't forget to rehearse any sound effects — they can really make the play come to life.

In the fisherman's play, we use a hand shadow as well as shadow puppets.

**FISHERMAN (P.9)**

**JEWELED FISH (P.22)**

**FLOWER (P.20)**

**SONG-BIRD (P.17)**

The birds are singing, the flowers are blooming, but the fisherman is not having much luck on the riverbank.

Suddenly the rod is almost jerked from his hand. He is sure it must be an enormous fish. He draws out a minnow.

The fisherman sighs and throws the fish back. From the depths of the river, a huge jeweled fish appears.

Its mighty jaws clamp over the fish and it dives back down to the depths .... pulling the poor fisherman with it!

# Tales and nursery rhymes

There really is no limit to the stories you can act out in shadow theater. Your characters can be anything you want them to be and they can do anything you want them to do. Transformation stories — where one creature turns into another — work very well in shadow theater because the audience doesn't see you making the change. But if you don't want to make up your own play, there are lots of fairytales and nursery rhymes you could choose from.

In this play we act out the nursery rhyme of Little Miss Muffet, using a jointed shadow puppet and the more simple spider. Remember to draw your scenery to suit your play.

MISS MUFFET (P.18)

SPIDER (P.15)

Little Miss Muffet
Sat on a tuffet,

Eating her curds and whey;

There came a big spider,

Who sat down beside her....
And frightened Miss Muffet away!

# Pattern help

Trace these shapes onto cardboard and cut out
to make the more complicated shadow puppets.

**ORCHESTRA (A,B,C,D)**

A

B

C

D

SONGBIRD (E,F)

E

F

SWINGING MONKEY
(G,H,1,J,K)

H

K

G

I

J

29

# Pattern help

## MISS MUFFET (A,B,C,D,E,F)

LION (G,H)

H

G

I

LION TAMER (I,J,K)

K

J

# Pattern help

DANCING CLOWN (A,B,C,D,E)